What Did Uncle Harold Know?

Tales from Bartenders

Jennifer Wood

Hirschwood Press
MILL VALLEY, CALIFORNIA

Copyright © 2016 by Jennifer Wood.

All rights reserved. No part of this publication may be reproduced, distributed or transmitted in any form or by any means, including photocopying, recording, or other electronic or mechanical methods, without the prior written permission of the publisher, except in the case of brief quotations embodied in critical reviews and certain other noncommercial uses permitted by copyright law. For permission requests, write to the publisher, addressed "Attention: Permissions Coordinator," at the address below.

Hirschwood Press
37 Bayview Terrace
Mill Valley CA 94941
talesfrombartenders.com

Publisher's Note: Names and other identifying details have been changed or omitted to protect confidentiality.

What Did Uncle Harold Know? / Jennifer Wood. —1st edition.
ISBN 978-0-9973749-0-2
Library of Congress Control Number: 2016935726

Grateful acknowledgment is made for permission to reprint the previously published material:

Copacabana (At The Copa)
Music by Barry Manilow
Lyric by Bruce Sussman and Jack Feldman
Copyright © 1978 by Universal Music – Careers, Appoggiatura Music and Camp Songs
All Rights Administered by Universal Music – Careers
International Copyright Secured All Rights Reserved
Reprinted by Permission of Hal Leonard Corporation

The "Awe" poem by Ace Remas, previously published in his book, *From the Back Porch* (Reno, Nevada: Jack Bacon and Company, 2009). Reprinted with permission of Ace Remas.

Excerpts from the November 2, 2014 "Barfly" column of Jeff Burkhart in the *Marin Independent Journal*. Reprinted by permission of Jeff Burkhart and the *Marin Independent Journal*.

The "Stained Glass" quote by Dr. Elisabeth Kubler-Ross. Reprinted by permission of the Elisabeth Kubler-Ross Family Limited Partnership.

For Betty
and
For my parents,
Ann Boutelle Mitchell Wood
Dr. Frank Boardman Wood

Contents

Introduction: Leap of Faith 1

HAROLD MITCHELL 13

CHRISTINE 21
Christine & Leroy 27
Christine's Tenderloin..31

BOBBIE... 35
A Nice Guy Named Dave...39
The Tilted Head 43
Steak and Lobster for the Masked Man.............................45
Freezing at the Workplace..47
Cook Bombs Restaurant, Steals Safe, Retains Job 49
When Darkness Falls...51

MRS. VANCE... 55
Mrs. Vance Outfoxes the Bartender 59
Can the Bartender Outfox Mrs. Vance?............................61
Mrs. Vance's Outfoxing Friend..63

MONICA... 67
Monica and the Cop 71

CHRISTINE & JEFF 79
An Addict Protects His Father 83
The Pacific Heights Lady 85
The Bloody Man in the Basement 87
Two Men in a Bar 89

NINA 93
The Shelter of Bars 97
The Vulnerability in Bars 101

SPREADING LIGHT 107
Aunt Ruby's 113

FACES AT THE BAR 117
A Mother's Love 123

MARK 131
Cowardice and Courage 137

ANN & XENA 141
Two Sisters Teach Each Other and a Town 145

ONE SUMMER IN MAINE 155
Mount Desert Island, Maine 159

LAST CALL 175
Acknowledgements 179
Notes 181
About the Author 185

Introduction: Leap of Faith

It takes moxie (and other things) to say to family, friends, and co-workers that you're writing a book, especially if it's your first book, no doubt your only book, and you haven't been trained.

Moxie. I like that word. *Webster's* defines it as "courage." *American Heritage* says it's "the ability to face difficulty with spirit." The word suggests grit, spunk, adventurousness. Moxie was my friend for much of my early life. Then it kind of retreated as the innocence and eagerness of youth collided with a few too many spirit-crushing issues. I'm writing this book, a book of bartender experiences and observations, because I believe people will be moved by the portrayal of human nature. I hope readers will laugh, recoil, and feel deeply about what they read. Each bartender I interviewed brought such emotions to me.

And, frankly, I'm writing this book because I want "my pal Moxie" to return to me. I have missed the passion and strength it used to give me—without even trying. It was just there. The thought of writing this book awakened my Moxie, propelled me through multiple interviews and hasn't let me down since.

I'd like to tell you about my former Moxie and how it connects with this book.

Moxie was with me when I went hitchhiking at the age of four. I grew up in the 1950s, in the small northern California town of Arcata (actually, Bayside, which was even smaller). My parents taught me about the dangers of hitchhiking. I apparently recognized it as a means of getting a desired ride. I remembered it when my five-year-old friend Susie and I snuck down the hill to get candy from the store at the bottom. We didn't feel like walking back up. Hitchhiking was my idea. A man responded right away to my little four-year-old thumb. Very fortunately, he took us home without incident. Always a good girl at heart, I confessed to my parents and

What Did Uncle Harold Know?

I got the worst punishment of my life. I never hitchhiked again. However, I have always liked how *enterprising* I was at so young an age.

Then there was the time when a high school counselor asked me at age 13 what I wanted to be when I grew up. That was back in the days when the standard female options were housewife, secretary, teacher, or nurse. I replied, "An actress!" The counselor reacted with an *isn't that so cute* smile. We locked eyes: "I mean it."

I know you're just itching to write down all my movies and plays since that moment.

You can put your pen down. But please don't turn away. Moxie and I simply took a career detour.

I received my bachelor's degree in June of 1972 and was marking time for my cousin to finish college. We had plans to travel throughout Europe for two to three months. I decided to live in Washington, D.C. while waiting for our August 1973 departure. That was a time when politics was considered honorable, when there was excitement and pride in the nation's capital, when things got done by the politicians. President Kennedy and his brother Bobby were lightning rods for millions of us. That was certainly true for me. In fact, one of my goals was to get to know members of the Kennedy family.

I didn't know anyone in Washington and was delighted when my letter addressed simply to "YWCA, Washington, D.C." yielded an inexpensive room there. The Y was an easy walk to the White House. I was screamingly excited. I would be arriving in January of 1973, in time to see the second inauguration of Richard Nixon and attend the Watergate trials.

I vividly recall Christmastime of 1972, a month before my departure. Our local newspaper carried a story about an automobile accident that had killed the young wife and baby daughter of a newly elected U.S. Senator from Delaware, Joseph R. Biden, Jr. His two- and three-year-old sons were fighting for their lives. They were out searching for a Christmas tree in Delaware when the accident occurred. The 30-year-old Senator was setting up his office on Capitol Hill. He was to be sworn in about the time I arrived.

I was so moved by the tragedy and showed the article to my mother. "I'm going to work for him, for this Senator Biden. I'll volunteer, maybe be his first intern. I'll combine it with a waitress job." Mom asked how I expected to meet Senator

Biden or his managers. I said I had no idea, but I would learn.

At last, mid-January 1973 arrived. And from the moment I landed in D.C. to the day in August when I left for Europe, magic dust seemed to sprinkle all over me.

I quit my first waitress job after only one week. It was a strange place. Otherwise, the job was the luck of my life. *The luck of my life.* The very first person I waited on inexplicably (he knew almost nothing about me) said he wanted to introduce me to his friend Suzanne Salinger, the 21-year-old daughter of President Kennedy's popular Press Secretary, Pierre Salinger. By March, Suzanne and I were becoming good friends. Her father (*Pierre Salinger!*) took us to dinner at a fancy restaurant. Henry Kissinger was there, said hello. Suzanne and I often got together for dinner or drinks until I left for Europe. We stayed in touch through the years. Then, in 1978, she and I flew up to Boston and drove to the Kennedy Compound in Hyannis Port. Her half-brother, who otherwise lived in Paris, France, was spending the summer with Ethel Kennedy, Robert Kennedy's widow, and her children. We ate dinner and spent the night at their house (*I stayed at the Kennedy Compound!*).

The next day, we all sailed on Nantucket Sound (*I went sailing with the Kennedys!*). Moxie was very, very happy with me.

In March 1973, two months after arriving in Washington, I called my parents with the news that I had gotten the job with Senator Biden. I would become his first unpaid Capitol Hill "intern," working weekends with his Administrative Assistant (Washington-speak for Chief of Staff), Wes Barthelmes. I can't remember how Wes and I met. I think I went up to Capitol Hill, found Senator Biden's office, walked through the open door, and there was Wes. And I told him what I had in mind (combine working there on weekends with my new waitress job) and Wes said Yes! My task was to help set up Senator Biden's office. Senator Biden was not there on weekends. He spent those days in Delaware while his little sons slowly recovered from their injuries.

I worked for months among pictures of the Biden family, the Senator, his boys, and his lovely wife and precious little girl. It was as if I worked in a huge mansion where I never saw the master. So I felt special delight when Wes asked me one summertime day if I would like to meet Senator Biden, to be placed on his schedule, before I left for Europe. Yes!

I was saving every penny for my two and a half months in Europe. I usually went to Capitol Hill by bus. But not this day, this day Senator Joseph Biden was waiting for me in his office. This day, etched into every part of me, I put on my best outfit and hailed a cab. The sun was shining brightly as I watched the Capitol dome come closer and closer to the undulating cab. I can still feel the tires. My eager eyes stared straight ahead. My face hurt from a bursting smile. Wes greeted me and ushered me into Senator Biden's office. I was 22. He was 30. I haven't the slightest idea what we talked about. But since neither of us has difficulty talking—no difficulty at all—the conversation easily flowed for about ten minutes.

When we were done, I walked down Capitol Hill to the Y. I had to work off my blazing energy. What a difference a few months can make. Rose petals fell from the sky.

The man who is now Vice President of the United States, Joe Biden, sent me a handwritten thank you note at the Y just before my departure.

My cousin's and my trip—ten countries in Western Europe—was grand. After an additional adventure or two, I returned to Washington. This time, in the fall of 1974, I was hired by Maine's senior Senator, Edmund S. Muskie. The first several months, I served as his receptionist and then, for the following four years, I handled writing and research projects. As further luck would have it, noted author Bernard Asbell had been assigned by Doubleday to write a book on the operations of the U.S. Senate. Senator Edmund S. Muskie (and his staff!) would be the primary focus. Bernie and I had several discussions during that initial receptionist period. *The Senate Nobody Knows* was finally published in 1978. Some universities assigned it for their political science courses.

I decided to try another work setting in 1979. Someone told me about an opening on the White House Staff, in the Advance Office of Vice President Walter Mondale. I landed the job. Damn! I coordinated logistics for Vice President Mondale's domestic and foreign travels. My office was in the ornate Old Executive Office Building next to the White House, but I was actually inside the White House every day for one reason or another. I flew on Air Force Two several times and rode in the corresponding motorcades.

What Did Uncle Harold Know?

Two of my former co-workers from Senator Muskie's office were working at the White House when I arrived. Their own lights shine brightly now: Madeleine Albright, the first female in American history to serve as Secretary of State; and Chris Matthews, host of MSNBC's long-running political program, *Hardball.*

I decided to move back to my home state of California in the early 1980s. Many good things have happened to me in the ensuing years—professionally and personally. But Washington career "sparkles" eluded me until I thought seriously about writing this book. I could instantly feel a passion and confidence—an energy—that I used to feel without effort. I think pizzazz is the wind beneath my wings.

I got on a roll. My newfound Moxie was ready for any issue, any fear or fight:

- Fear of criticism—you wrote this? **Yuck!**
  At least I stepped into the arena!
- Fear of failure—Don't quit your day job:
  Didn't!
- Who will publish it?
  Me! Self-publishing is great.
- Who will distribute it?
  Me! My family! Here's one for you.

Sometimes things are so simple.

Then I hit a snag—of my own non-moxie making. Suddenly the part I thought would be the easiest—interviewing bartenders—became daunting. What bartenders? What bars? I can't just walk into a busy bar and interrupt. Where will we otherwise meet? What if the bartender is a serial killer? I sought bars from dives to fancy. How can I possibly set up a dive bar interview? Am I a dive bar kind of gal? I hate this.

My book is getting on my nerves. **Help Me, Moxie.**

Then along came Lee, a woman I know from work. My ears perked up like an eager puppy when she just happened to mention that her beloved, beautifully educated daughter Christine, from affluent Marin County, California, chose to live in the Tenderloin district of San Francisco. She then added—without prompting—that her daughter also *worked* in the Tenderloin. As a bartender.

Her daughter Christine works as a bartender in the Tenderloin!

My emotions zoomed from sympathy for Lee (this was clearly not her favorite subject) to exquisite joy and relief for me. Is that awful? I hope not. When you read Christine's contributions to this book, your emotions will be full. I was going to thank Moxie for kicking in just when I needed it, but I know the magic belongs to Christine and Lee.

After Christine and I talked in San Francisco, I *knew* the book had truly begun. I drove my shiny new red car home, over the Golden Gate Bridge. I looked at the beautiful boats undulating on San Francisco Bay and screamed, Uncle Harold! Our book is actually going to happen. I can feel it. I just know it! Are you ready, Uncle Harold? Here we go, Uncle Harold, here we go!

HAROLD MITCHELL

Uncle Harold will not be contributing to this book in the manner you might expect. In fact, he died more than twenty years ago, without my ever laying eyes on him or ever asking him a single one of my many questions. What a waste. Then again, had we talked, this book probably wouldn't exist. I'll explain.

Harold J. Mitchell was my great-uncle. My grandfather, James E. Mitchell, was his older brother. The two Mitchell boys and their three sisters grew up in the poor Irish section of Bangor, Maine. My grandfather was determined to set a different course for himself. James was the first in the family to go to college. A scholarship student, he received a bachelor's from Bowdoin in only *three* years and was valedictorian. Harvard Law School followed, then marriage into one of Bangor's most prestigious families. He established his own law firm. His wife, my future grandmother, was Elizabeth ("Betty") Boutelle Palmer, the vibrant, extraordinarily talented granddaughter of Bangor's most famous Civil War hero and later U.S. Congressman, Charles Addison Boutelle. My grandparents had five children. The first was named Ann Boutelle. She is my mother.

Uncle Harold's life was very different. He never went to college. He never married nor had children. He didn't grow up to live in a big house in one of the finest sections of Bangor. However, like his big brother, Harold found his calling and spent his adulthood excelling at it. Uncle Harold was a bartender.

A bartender. I always smile at that. What an interesting job.

And Uncle Harold wasn't just any bartender. He hit the big-time. His career was defined by working at—and sometimes heading up—the bars of two of the most famous nightclubs in 20th century America, the original Copacabana in New York City and the original Sands Hotel in Las Vegas. These were the places where future headliners made their debuts. Performing at "The Copa" was considered the pinnacle of show business success, and featured such luminaries as Tony Bennett, Nat King Cole, Harry Belafonte, Jerry Lewis & Dean Martin, Sammy Davis, Jr., and The Supremes. The Sands Hotel in its heyday was the center of entertainment in Las Vegas. It was there that the "Rat Pack" of Frank Sinatra, Dean Martin, Sammy Davis, Jr., Peter Lawford, Joey Bishop—and their female "mascots" such as Shirley MacLaine—established Vegas as "The Entertainment Capital of the World." Harold Mitchell from Bangor, Maine presided among them and their fans.

If you haven't thought about it much, you might think a successful bartender's talents consist of mixing good drinks and handling the pace of a busy bar. Dealing with the public, rowdy or obnoxious, also comes to mind. Uncle Harold could easily handle all of that.

Then I think about the quiet warmth I'm told Uncle Harold exuded, he with his premature shock of gray-white hair highlighting his forever dark, thick eyebrows. His twinkling Irish eyes, inviting you in to share a story, a sorrow, a secret. A laugh or two. The kind of guy the average Joe and Jill enjoys, the kind a celebrity, away from home, could relax and chat with after hours. This is a bartender who creates an atmosphere, draws a crowd and keeps people coming. These talents make all the difference. Uncle Harold had them.

I often wonder what his customers talked to him about, what he observed, what he learned about human nature. I wonder about his impact on the lives of his customers, as well as theirs on him.

Sadly, Uncle Harold is no longer with us, so we will never learn from him what he experienced, what he knew, after a long career bartending.

I decided if we can't hear from my great-uncle, why not interview other bartenders from a variety of establishments, and learn from them? I have been interviewing such bartenders for several months. The upcoming pages hold their answers. I hope you will be as moved as I am.

Like liquid fire
the music ran –
And so the dance began.

~Grace Hodsdon Boutelle

Excerpt from
Copacabana (At The Copa)

~Barry Manilow, Jack Feldman, Bruce Sussman

Her name was Lola, she was a showgirl
With yellow feathers in her hair
and a dress cut down to there
She would merengue and do the cha-cha
But while she tried to be a star,
Tony always tended bar
Across the crowded floor,
they worked from 8 till 4
They were young and they had each other
Who could ask for more?

At the Copa, Copacabana
The hottest spot north of Havana
At the Copa, Copacabana
Music and passion were always the fashion
At the Copa…they fell in love.

CHRISTINE

Christine is the first person I interview for this book. She is the daughter of one of my work acquaintances. She suggests we talk at a quiet tea house on Bush Street in San Francisco.

She looks as I expected. She is slender, with a lovely face and with her mother's radiant smile. She is warm and articulate. Her fully tattooed arms and legs offer the only suggestion of lifestyle choices that might differ from other well-educated twenty-somethings from affluent Marin County, a few miles north, just across the Golden Gate Bridge. I also realize "body art" is all the rage among all sorts of people.

I am prepared for an education on life in the Tenderloin district of San Francisco. Christine told me when we first talked that she lived and worked there. She wants to live and work there. She discloses that she "hit bottom" with alcohol and other drug addictions while bartending at one of the seedier Tenderloin bars. She also got clean and sober while continuing to bartend there. That place has since closed.

These days, Christine mostly works as a job counselor for the disabled. Despite this, she insists on continuing to reside in the Tenderloin and on bartending one night a week at another bar in that area. She tells me that observing the physical and emotional deterioration caused by alcohol and drug abuse keeps her from returning to those behaviors. She sees the waste of lives put on hold. She speaks of "the procrastinating of life" produced by addictions. Christine describes how the addict's "world becomes smaller." Each day, all day, life becomes only about where to drink or score drugs, needles, and a fix. Single Room Occupancy housing provides a place to sleep. Then the world becomes a two-block radius—the places to sleep, drink, and obtain and take drugs.

I am riveted by what Christine now tells me. Her description of the Tenderloin bar where she worked for several years, the one that is now closed, ignites grotesque feelings about the bar's sights and smells. The carpeting throughout the place, including the restroom, was soaked with alcohol and urine, sometimes accompanied by dog excrement. The owners refused to pay for critically needed plumbing work, leading to problems so bad that "shit water" came from the faucets.

Why, I wonder, would anyone, much less this feminine, intelligent young woman, spend a minute in such a place? I think of her appealing mother. Did she and Christine's father know about all this? If so, how did they cope?

What on earth draws Christine to *still* want to live and work in the Tenderloin? I'm just not grasping it.

I am also intrigued by the unexpected focus of this first bartender interview. I had told Christine at the outset that the stories the bartenders told me, whatever they might be, would determine the direction of my book. I had anticipated hearing the secrets drunken *bar customers* would tell bartenders—murders, burglaries, having a secret second family—that kind of disclosure. Christine was taking me into the *bartender's* world and, in this case, the netherworld of an upper-middle-class, educated woman. I loved the unexpected trajectory. I could now feel that the life of lovely Christine and her Tenderloin world would offer unique, and profound, material for my book. I also knew I had some learning to do. I needed more information to develop insights and empathy for all that Christine was telling me.

Here we go.

A heart that can recognize, without aid of the eyes, the gifts that life holds for the wise

~Verse from a poem the Irish Ambassador to the United States recited to President Kennedy in 1961, to honor the birth of John F. Kennedy, Jr.

Christine & Leroy

Christine is eager to tell me about a man named Leroy. Her tender feelings for him are palpable. "I will always love Leroy," she says.

To understand Christine's decision to leave the trappings of an upper-middle-class life, it helps to get to know Leroy. He is now 80 years old. Christine says he was "a grandfather to everyone," "a quintessential old man" to inhabitants of the seedy Tenderloin bar in San Francisco that was her place of employment for several years. I use the word "inhabitants" because Leroy and others practically lived there. They drank all day long. Leroy even finished leftover drinks so they "wouldn't go to waste."

The bar owners welcomed Leroy. He did some chores for them and sometimes got free drinks. But the owners and Christine also knew Leroy was their "Mascot"—a character, a moneymaker for them. He drew a crowd. Indeed, Leroy became somewhat legendary. People would go to the bar just to see his warm, craggy face and hear him spin tales. He could read a crowd. He knew how to connect with people and make them laugh.

He railed against injustice, especially towards "the underdog." He was not Jewish, but the plight of Jews especially bothered him. And he loved to talk about his friend Alfredo, married-with-children Alfredo, who lived in Mexico. He talked about him all the time, how he'd sent him money and presents. Everyone at the bar quietly understood that Leroy was in love.

Leroy was regarded at the bar as a "brilliant" man. He was a former teacher from parts unknown, and lived off money from investments. He told Christine and others that his penchant for feeding pigeons (and any other hungry animal, even when he would benefit from the food himself) would have landed him "in the gulag" in his former country. He never mentioned Russia, nor did any accent betray his origins. Whenever Christine tried to get to know him better by asking him personal questions, he would immediately change the subject.

Through the years, no matter how many times he ranted about injustice, and no matter his obvious decline from drinking and dementia and aging, nothing dampened Leroy's spirit. His delighted cries of "good-good-good!" still rang through the bar. And he kept on telling his bar family, "We may not win, but we never lose!" And he told them not to worry, "You always come out smelling like a rose."

Christine taught me that bar customers can profoundly affect the trajectory and meaning of a bartender's life. That is what Leroy did for Christine. That is what the people of the Tenderloin do for Christine.

Christine's Tenderloin

If Leroy was The Mascot and Maestro of the bar, Christine was his counterpart in a different sort of way. She was also a big moneymaker for the owners. She had her fans. Sales flew upwards with her arrival. What's a pretty, educated young woman doing here, bartending in a place like this? Some people said the bar reminded them of the popular old TV show, *Cheers*. It could have that flavor: a bunch of people regularly gathering together, a "bar family" drinking and having fun at their local bar "living room."

There was a glaring difference. Christine's "bar family" was comprised of people so alcohol- and drug-addicted, so down on their luck, so unkempt, that many otherwise kind and tolerant San Franciscans might readily recoil and cross the street, if encountering them. As the years went by, even Leroy's hygiene diminished to the point that Christine found it difficult to hug him.

Still, this was Christine's Tenderloin. For her, it was where people "don't have the energy to be phony, where they are unapologetically themselves."

I am told by a woman I meet, a woman born of privilege, that she understands the attraction of the Tenderloin. She works there, too, on issues pertaining to the homeless, the addicted, traumatized war survivors. There is "an edge to life" in that world, she says, a realness and daily drama, where the inhabitants become a cohesive group. They stick together, thoughtfully protecting one another. If someone kicks alcohol or other drug addictions, there can still be a "vicarious pull" towards staying in that intense world. The inhabitants often display wellsprings of genuine kindness and caring towards one another. This contrasts with what can be an indifferent and hostile world outside, a world populated by self-absorbed people wrapped in competing facades.

What Did Uncle Harold Know?

People who are like Christine seem to respond instinctively to everyone as a *human being, a person.* They see what lies beneath rough and tough exteriors. They *get, and do not forget,* how easy it could be for *any of us* to degenerate if left to live on the street, with few toilets and places to wash, when financially devastated by a job loss or medical crisis, people rejecting you. Alcohol and other drugs can then work their malice.

I see that Christine has a gift. It is her heart. Those who drifted into her Tenderloin bar, or were inspired to return, no doubt felt it. She responded to everyone with respect and genuine interest and caring. Affection. Imagine how that must have felt.

One of my favorite Leroy and Christine stories involves his hair. She shows me a picture of his hair, which is ample but not long. A huge head of hair; an envy of the bald and balding. "He cut it a little every day," Christine says. Rather than combing it or using gel on the hairs that can stick up in the morning, Leroy used clippers. Christine knew he couldn't see how matted his hair was in the back. She knew it would trouble him. "So I'd take a wet cloth and try to smooth it for him." She knew he would like that. She wanted to do that for him.

*Awe arrives, to astound and delight
in an instant,
as in the distance a flash of
lightning illumines the landscape
moments ago hidden in darkness.
Then, clarity disappears and the
revealed is only remembered,
a mere shadow of what was seen,
like thunder rolling across valley
and range to slowly diminish to a
complete absence.
Did I imagine the lightning strike?
We try to remember such insights,
to classify and to record
so that we might revive the awe
in lesser moments.
So it is with our lives.*

~Ace Remas

BOBBIE

Sometimes I received bartender stories from the most unexpected people in the most unexpected places. I just casually told a manager in a business totally unrelated to bars or restaurants that I was writing this book. She looked at me and laughed. She had bartended and managed restaurants for years. In fact, she was now working in this new industry in large part to get away from that drama. I asked what she meant.

Fasten your seat belts. Here's Bobbie.

Courage is grace under pressure.

~Ernest Hemingway

A Nice Guy Named Dave

Back in the 1980s, Bobbie was having a good time managing a bar and restaurant off Highway 80 in northern California. It was known for Cajun food, but also served steak and fish. The bar was fun. Lots of folks used it as their stopping-off place en route to or from Lake Tahoe.

Bobbie recalls the bar and restaurant owners, a husband and wife, hired a man to help them remodel their house. They liked David Rundle and hired him as the handyman for their business as well. People found him reliable, a good guy. Funny how the owners' dog barked up a storm every time Dave came around. You know how some dogs can be!

Dave was in his early thirties and about Bobbie's age. His cute surfer looks caught her eye. Heck, Bobbie thought—more than once—if I hadn't gotten married, I might pursue him!

The owners had a policy against female employees leaving the bar and restaurant alone after dark. Dave offered to escort Bobbie and the other gals to their cars as their shifts ended. He made them feel safe. They appreciated Dave, especially now that the news was full of serial killer stories. Women living and working near bustling Highway 80 were becoming increasingly alarmed. Female bodies were being dumped along the roadside. Other murders and rapes in different parts of California and in Texas seemed the work of the same man, according to the authorities.

The owners stepped up enforcement of their female protection policy. Dave Rundle spent months safeguarding Bobbie and the other women.

Relief at last spread throughout California when authorities announced they had caught the killer. They were confident they had their man.

With time, they were proven right: a jury found him guilty and sentenced him to death.

What Did Uncle Harold Know?

Bobbie and the bar and restaurant crew still think about the day they heard the name of the man the police arrested. "No Way!"—they can still hear themselves say. "How could it possibly be?"—they still think. They wrack their brains for the clues, the red flags, they missed. Nothing makes sense. What they do know, and know for sure, is that they will never forget the name of the man who got arrested and sentenced to death, David Allen Rundle.

The Tilted Head

"Picture this!" exclaims Bobbie, about a steakhouse she managed in Honolulu when she was only 26. It was a wonderful restaurant—authentic thatched roof, gorgeous views, delicious food.

Then one night, just about closing time, three strangers burst in, their guns drawn.

In a split second, one gun pressed against the temple of an employee who'd grabbed her phone. Another aimed at the three customers at the bar. Bobbie could feel the metal of the third at the back of her neck. "Give me all your cash."

She tried to stay cool, even casual. Maintaining eye contact, her fingers waltzed frantically under the counter for the silent alarm. She couldn't find it.

Just then, she turned her head, ever so slightly, kind of a tilt. She doesn't know why. A shot rang out, hitting her face. Blood spewed everywhere. "This is how I will die," Bobbie remembers thinking as she slid to the floor.

Head wounds are known to bleed. A lot. They can make a minor injury seem more traumatic. This time, Bobbie got lucky; the bullet only grazed her cheek. Full impact had only been a tilt away, the doctors later said.

Bobbie smiles as she remembers how the cops got the emergency call. The silent alarm stared right at her as she lay on the floor. She pressed it.

People have asked Bobbie through the years how that night affected her. Is she anxious, hardened? They ask her why she tilted her head.

She is quick to respond. She has no specific idea why she moved her head just in time, why she was spared. But she is convinced there is a Plan for all of us. She's been spared several times since that night, close calls in other restaurants. Her face lights up. "I'm still here!"

Steak and Lobster for the Masked Man

A mere six months after Bobbie was shot, a man wearing a ski mask burst into the same Honolulu restaurant, put a gun to her head, and demanded all the money. Bobbie stared straight ahead, locking eyes with the stricken bartender. She told him to get the money. He did. Then Bobbie did something she can't quite believe. Bet the bartender and customers will never forget.

Just as the masked man was leaving, Bobbie politely asked, "Would you like our steak and lobster dinner, too?"

What! Burglar Etiquette? Was Bobbie losing it?

She chuckles. She's not sure what was up with her. "I think I wanted to give him everything I could think of so he wouldn't shoot me, so he'd take the money and run."

He took the money and ran.

Skipped dinner. Maybe he didn't like fish.

Freezing at the Workplace

Ever had a bad day at work? Want to yell, "I'm out of here. I hate this place!" Ever been the boss wanting to scream, "What other manager has to deal with stuff like this? I've been shot, held up—and now this!"

Bobbie recalls another day in her bar and restaurant career. She was managing a popular small-town steakhouse. There was an eerie silence as she entered the premises one day. Where was everyone? She called out. Frantically looking around, she rushed toward noises in the freezer room. She found what she was looking for. Her staff was there. *Stuffed inside the freezers.*

Turns out the burglars got away with all the money and were never caught. As for her staff, they all made it out of the freezers alive—some in better shape than others. Frozen meat would never look the same.

Cook Bombs Restaurant, Steals Safe, Retains Job

Bobbie arrived at work one day to find the restaurant and bar she managed dynamited on one side. Just blasted away. The safe was gone. She figures it contained at least $10,000. The FBI was called in. Their investigation came up empty.

Word around the restaurant, however, confident word, was that the cook and his jailbird brother did it. Bobbie looked to the owner for leadership and protection. He decided to look the other way. Who knows for sure what happened? Besides, good cooks around these parts are hard to find.

When Darkness Falls

Bobbie will never forget that fierce snowstorm, the one that knocked out power lines, closed roads, and stranded people in the Sierras, where she was now working. Even the popular restaurant up the hill had to close for two days.

Bobbie's restaurant was different, had much better access. She and the owner, Bill, knew that visitors to the town and locals who couldn't get home needed a place to park themselves, get a bite to eat, to drink. The snowploughs would take time. Bill and Bobbie decided to keep the restaurant open, even without electricity. They figured they had enough light to function during the day. It was still early.

They had to get creative, and fast. People were lining up. Key restaurant workers were snowed out. The cook, bartender and servers had to be replaced. Bill figured he could use the gas grill to salvage as much perishable food as possible. Bobbie had years of bartending experience, so she dashed behind the bar. She even convinced her firefighter husband to wash dishes. Two waiters from the closed hilltop restaurant offered their services. Everyone genuinely wanted to help, but they weren't dumb. This was the only show in town and they saw dollar signs! They weren't wrong. The place was packed all day—everyone laughing, talking, drinking. When darkness fell, Bill and Bobbie announced it was time to go. They assured an early opening the next day.

Their luck continued that second day. The crowd returned. And just as nighttime lurked and they'd have to close, their electricity came on. Other establishments remained dark, so the nighttime business was all theirs.

Bill and Bobbie knew the bar and restaurant business well. People unfamiliar with it might be amazed at what goes on. You hear stories about the well-known chef who started crying—literally weeping—on a busy night when one of his carefully prepared meals was sent back by an irate customer. Then there's the server who shuddered remembering the customer who asked for seven—and he meant seven—french fries to accompany his entrée. The chef thought the request so funny that he gave him eight—and oh! the server and restaurant patrons will not soon forget the red-faced screaming of the man when he counted to eight. Things can get argumentative, competitive, strange. Bobbie, of all people, knew things could get way worse than that. Hell, she'd had a gun aimed at her head, been shot in the face, had her staff stuffed in freezers! You develop a lot of unexpected skills managing a bar and restaurant.

When the storm lifted and things calmed down, Bobbie and Bill steeled themselves for what they'd find. Or not find. They were already amazed there had been no break-ins or fights.

They searched all over the place. They could find nothing wrong. They still talk about those two snowy days. The crisis seemed to bring out the best in everybody. People pulled together, pooled resources, and had fun. The way life should be.

*Life is short and we do not have too
much time for gladdening the
hearts of those who are traveling
the dark journey with us.
Oh be swift to love!
Make haste to be kind.*

~Henri Frederic Amiel

MRS. VANCE

As I waited for several bartenders to organize their thoughts and tell me their tales, I realized I had good stories of my own to share. I'd never been a bartender, but readily recalled some *very interesting evenings* out drinking and eating with friends. I am very pleased that my friend—to be known here as "Mrs. Vance"—laughed with delight when I told her what I planned to tell you. Get ready!

We ought never to do wrong when people are looking.

~Mark Twain

Mrs. Vance Outfoxes the Bartender

Who would think that a "game" goes on, a game with some regularity, between a bartender and a bar patron?

Please meet my friend, Mrs. Vance. She is a sophisticated lady, the former wife of a big philanthropist, a big-time CEO. Big money. She's a great gal, I sometimes have to tell a bartender. But She Does Not Suffer Fools. *Do not lie to Mrs. Vance.*

You Will Lose.

Such was a night at a fine restaurant in Marin County, California when Mrs. Vance ordered a Rusty Nail. She always, and I do mean always, orders Kettle One Vodka Martinis. Dry. Ice on the side. I focused closely on this aberration. I did not know what a Rusty Nail was at that moment. *I know now.* Everyone in the restaurant knows *forever*. The bartender will surely never, never, never again do what he did that warm summer night when my friend, Mrs. Vance, branched out from her usual Kettle One Vodka Martini and ordered a Rusty Nail.

It's all about Drambuie. Most Rusty Nail connoisseurs would argue there are few (actually no) respectable substitutions for Drambuie. I do not remember what the bartender decided to **secretly** use as a substitute when he discovered the bar was out of Drambuie that night. But I am sure he will never, never, never do that again. For, you see, Mrs. Vance noticed, **noticed**, that Drambuie was missing from her drink. She questioned the waitress, somewhat gently, and the waitress checked with the bartender. Do not tell Mrs. Vance, "Of course, your Rusty Nail was made with Drambuie," when you know it was not. People like Mrs. Vance *Know*.

Unpleasant words were exchanged. Mrs. Vance asked to see the bottle of Drambuie.

Oops.

Many apologies. No charge for the drink.

Can the Bartender Outfox Mrs. Vance?

Here's a good one. Not long after the Rusty Nail evening, Mrs. Vance and three other friends went out to dinner at another restaurant in Marin County. They all had martinis, straight up. Standard martini glasses. All was good. Everything was beautiful until the second round of martinis arrived. One of the four martini glasses appeared to be considerably smaller than the other three. Guess who got the little one? Mrs. Vance was not happy, not happy at all. Carlos, the server, was immediately beckoned. He cheerfully explained that all of the desired glasses were in use, but not to worry; both types had equal volume. Mrs. Vance did not believe him. Her friends offered to switch drinks with her, but that did not help. She drank vodka; her friends, gin. She also wanted that little glass with the smaller pour to *disappear*. **Do not try to fool Mrs. Vance OR her friends.**

Carlos scrambled to locate a clean glass in the style Mrs. Vance desired. He brought it to the table. Mrs. Vance and her friends watched as he poured the untouched vodka from the "little" glass into the new one. Slowly, slowly he poured, until every drop was gone. Ha! It filled the *entire* "big" glass. A triumphant Carlos exclaimed, "See! Just as I told you. How do you say, 'optical illusion?' You just think it is smaller—there is no big glass or small glass."

Mrs. Vance and her friends were truly amazed.

Mrs. Vance thanked Carlos for his demonstration. She laughed and shook her head. No one could believe it.

"Carlos," Mrs. Vance announced. "It doesn't matter. From now on, only give me the big glass," she said pointing to her new one.

"Always the big glass," Carlos assured her.

Mrs. Vance's Outfoxing Friend

I had a waitress job at a Washington, D.C. restaurant many years ago. That was back in the days of the "three martini lunches" popular with executives. One middle-aged guy ate lunch there every day. People said he was a prominent architect. He looked like a worn out used car salesman to me, but what did I know? I'd just turned 21, the legal drinking age, and was new to the restaurant/bar business. The architect arrived with a different female every day. Each one had the unmistakable *Lady of the Evening* look.

One noontime, the architect beckoned me to his table for his usual martini order. "Jenny," he slurred, "We'll take extra, extra, extra dry Beefeater Martinis, straight up, with no vegetables. Can you do that for us, Honey?"

I had no sooner ordered and delivered the drinks, when his voice rang out, "Jenny! I asked for dry; extra, extra, extra dry. There's way too much vermouth. Don't you agree, Sweetheart?" *"Way too much,"* his companion purred. They demanded new drinks.

The restaurant was busy. The bartender shot angry eyes at me when I returned the drinks. "That jerk is just showing off. There's no vermouth at all. I'm not making new drinks."

The bartender saw my worried look. "You gotta learn to fake it, Jenny. Wait here for a while, then take the same drinks back to them."

"Really?" "Yes, Jenny, really." His tone let me know, unmistakably, that I had better wise up fast. I did.

While I pretended new drinks were being mixed, I practiced how to deliver them without anxiety:

"You'll love these!!"

(Wait! What if they realize they're the originals?)

"Dry as a bone now!"

(No! They were that way before; what if they ask for details?)

What Did Uncle Harold Know?

"Here you go!" Ha! A line so neutral, so perfect!

In no time, I delivered that line with gusto, then feigned supreme confidence as I watched the architect test the "new" martini.

"Ah, Jenny! This is so much better! Don't you think, Sweetheart?"

"Sooo much better," his companion cooed.

In the forty years that have passed since that moment, on the rare occasions when I have sent a drink or meal back, I have made certain that the replacement is *actually* different from the original. When asked by the server if everything is okay now, I still find myself pausing, hesitating…before giving a response. I still hear the gales of laughter erupting from my co-workers and me as we watched the architect and his lady leave the restaurant.

*Do not try to fool
even a reluctant outfoxer!*

~Yours truly, the author

MONICA

A friend told me about a bartender in Auburn, California, named Monica. Monica frequently served a local law enforcement officer at her bar. His name was in the news because he was investigating two especially gruesome murders. My friend said Monica tried to make her bar a place of relaxation and comfort for him during those awful months. She suggested I contact her for this book.

I'm glad I met Monica. She taught me even more about the emotional dynamics that can flow between a bartender and a bar customer. Here is what happened.

*Try to be a rainbow
in someone's cloud.*

~Maya Angelou

Monica and the Cop

The city of Auburn rests in the heart of Northern California's famous Gold Country. It is located some thirty miles from the state capital of Sacramento, with a population just shy of 13,000. It is bordered by the lovely American River Canyon and situated in the western foothills of the Sierra Nevada Mountains. Auburn is the county seat of Placer County. Tourists are invited to enjoy the vibrancy of the city, from historic downtown to the variety of shops and restaurants it offers.

Auburn and neighboring towns are also places that have known dreadful crimes over the years. Murders in a small town can upset inhabitants in a unique way. There is a sense that you actually know the victims—or the perpetrators. Maybe both. News accounts mention familiar streets and local businesses, locations where the victim lived or worked or met his or her demise. You learn what high school the victim once attended, and you realize that was your school, too. Or your cousin once dated his sister. Familiarity. It adds a sense of involvement and drama to news that is already horrific.

Monica has lived and bartended around Auburn for decades. She likes living there but is also attuned to the underbelly of the city. She wants to talk to me about two Auburn area murders that occurred in the early 1980s. She reminds me that author Joan Merriam wrote an acclaimed book, *Little Girl Lost*, about the first crime she discusses. I recall the case. It was well publicized and especially shocking because it involved two teenage girls, who were only 14 and 15 years old. They were the killers. They murdered an 85-year-old woman named Anna Brackett in her home just outside Auburn in 1983. The girls didn't know her; they told authorities they randomly selected her house. Mrs. Brackett was happy to let them in to use her phone and get a drink of water—ruses to get inside. She told them she had a grandson just about their age.

Then the girls slaughtered her with 28 stabs. "It was a lot of fun," one of them later said. The girls said their motive was simply to do something they'd never done before; others suggest they "finally vented on another as helpless as themselves."

Jurors were not swayed by reports of the neglect and abuse the girls had known their entire lives. They were given the maximum sentence for juveniles. One of the girls was held for nine years, the other for twelve. Both have been free since the mid-1990s.

They ended Anna Brackett's life in 1983. The kind and beloved woman died a trusting woman; she never saw it coming.

Monica did not know any of the people involved in that crime. She thought of it, though, as she prepared to talk to me about another shocking crime that hit the Auburn news in 1980, a few years before Mrs. Brackett was murdered. This time Monica knew someone involved. He was a cop investigating the case. He often went to her bar. She saw him in the news and she saw him sitting right before her throughout the ordeal. She knew he couldn't talk in any depth or detail about the case, so she did her best just to provide a place of normalcy and comfort for him. Sometimes laughter.

Monica knew from the news that two people had been murdered, Eric Hanson and his girlfriend, Catherine Blount. They were killed at their home in Ophir, a couple of miles from Auburn. Monica wanted me to investigate the details of the case, and to understand why she felt such sympathy and admiration for the cop.

Here's what happened. In September of 1980, according to court documents (United States Court of Appeals for the Ninth Circuit; Mickey v. Ayers), Douglas Scott Mickey "lived on an Air Force base in Japan with his wife, [a lieutenant] who worked as a nurse, and her two children. Mickey did not have a job and his family was experiencing financial difficulties. On September 17, 1980, Mickey flew to California, his home state. He stayed with Edward Rogers, a longtime friend. Mickey disclosed to Rogers that he traveled to California in order to rob and murder Eric Lee Hanson. After that, Mickey planned to travel to Alaska to kill his wife's ex-husband in order to obtain life insurance proceeds for his wife and children, who were beneficiaries under the policy. Although Hanson, a drug dealer, was a longtime friend of his, Mickey had a grudge against him. Mickey believed that Hanson had stolen some of Mickey's personal property...."

In spite of his murderous plans, Douglas Mickey spent a night at the home of Eric Hanson and his girlfriend, Catherine Blount. Things must have seemed okay to those two. They invited Mickey back into their home when he knocked on their door several days later. This time, Mickey used his own knife and a pistol supplied by Edward Rogers and brutally murdered them.

He stole substantial property as he fled the house, driving away in Hanson's Volkswagen. He wiped everything clean of fingerprints. He then met up with Edward Rogers and gave him the stolen property. They stashed the goods and ditched the Volkswagen. Mickey decided to escape to Japan.

It took just a few days for authorities to catch up with Rogers and secure a statement from him. He disclosed what they had done in exchange for immunity.

The Japanese government refused to waive extradition and kept Douglas Mickey in prison in their country until early 1981. But on January 12, 1981, a U.S. Federal Marshal, a sheriff, and a detective from California arrived in Japan with an extradition warrant. These were the men who brought Douglas Scott Mickey back to California to face charges in the deaths of Eric Lee Hanson and Catherine Blount. These were the men who ensured Mickey would be held accountable in an American court. He received the death penalty. The cop from Monica's bar was one of these men.

Monica taught me another way a bar and bartender can help customers. Think of the pressures law enforcement officers feel, the horrors they see. The information they have to absorb. Think of the methods they need to devise and discover to help them cope. Most of us can't even imagine it.

As this cop tried to relax with a drink or two at his local bar, at Monica's bar, these facts must have pummeled his head and later disturbed his sleep: one day Douglas Mickey spent an evening socializing with two friends at their home. He spent the night with them. A few days later, he visited them again. This time, according to official crime reports, Mickey "bludgeoned his longtime friend [Eric] with a baseball bat and slit his throat ear to ear, down to his spinal cord" because of a "grudge." He then stabbed Eric's girl-

What Did Uncle Harold Know?

friend seven times, with three blows piercing her heart.

Eric and Catherine innocently opened their door. Horror walked inside.

*Even in our sleep,
pain which cannot forget
falls drop by drop upon the heart
until, in our own despair,
against our will, comes wisdom
through the awful grace of God.*

~Aeschylus

CHRISTINE & JEFF

I am surprised and intrigued that, so far, no bartender has told me what I had anticipated would dominate our discussions: shocking secrets divulged by bar patrons to their bartenders.

I discuss the issue with Christine, the first bartender I interviewed. She responds with a warm smile, "I wouldn't tell you if I knew any." Her tone is thoughtful. She explains she would never violate the trust shown to her, even if identities were kept confidential.

I'm pleased that she feels comfortable discussing three especially emotional occurrences at the notorious Tenderloin bar where she bartended for years. I discern a theme threading through these stories that somehow reminds me of a recent newspaper column. In that column, the columnist—who is also a bartender—Jeff Burkhart, describes an interaction between two men at his upscale bar. His story, at first glance, is very different from what Christine shares with me. And each of Christine's stories differs from one another. How odd, I think, that I find a connection among all of them.

Then Buddha came along and it all made sense.

We are what we think.
All that we are
arises with our thoughts.
With our thoughts,
we make our world.

~**Buddha**

An Addict Protects His Father

Christine first tells me about a man, a regular at the bar, who was a meth addict. William was constantly in and out of jail. Christine assumes the charges against him involved drugs, but she never inquired. She tells me she has learned in her bartending career, "Don't ask questions you don't want the answers to. There's a reason people end up in the Tenderloin."

One day, William came into the bar all sweaty and asked her to do him a favor. He was desperate, claiming the police were after him and wanted to confiscate all his belongings. He asked Christine to safeguard his most important possession, the urn he held in his arms, an urn filled with his father's ashes.

She said, "No way."

Christine knew he might be telling the truth, or suffering from drug-related paranoia. She also questioned what was actually in the urn. He removed the lid and they inspected it together. It was filled with ashes.

William's pleas were so urgent she decided to take it. She hid it in a safe place at the bar. The ashes remained there for months, without word from William. Then one day his brother unexpectedly appeared. He asked Christine for the urn; he would protect the ashes now.

Two brothers thus honored their father. A bartender lent them a hand.

The Pacific Heights Lady

Christine now focuses on the variety of "sex problems exhibited at bars"—cheating spouses, people paying for sex, not using protection, women going home with complete strangers from the seediest places.

She especially remembers an older, wealthy white woman who drove her fancy car to the notorious Tenderloin bar. The lady had a penchant for young black men, and regularly picked them up. She paid for their food and drinks and bought them clothes. She took them to her home in affluent Pacific Heights. She appeared to pay for "friendships" that would also bring her sexual favors. People at the bar talked about her.

Christine and the rest of us can only speculate about the woman's motives and needs, about why she would take such risks to her reputation, her health, and to her very life.

Christine suggests that perhaps she was a woman of a certain age with a repressed sexuality. Perhaps she achieved some curious validation in her successful quest to attract young men. Maybe she was tired of the double standard, and the "cougar" element of older woman/younger man gave her a special charge—the same with the white/black element. Maybe she was simply attracted to young black men and decided to go for it.

She could expect not to run into people of her social status at that particular bar. If she did, that would say something about them as well. There was safety in that.

She was, for sure, a woman who took breathtaking risks to realize her fantasies and meet her needs.

The Bloody Man in the Basement

The owner of Christine's bar was friends with a man known to have a serious anger problem. He showed up at the bar on several occasions covered in blood. Christine does not know exactly why and learned not to ask.

She and her co-workers also learned to quickly comply with the owner's command when the bloody man raced into the bar: hide him! He was taken to the kitchen to wash and then spirited off to the basement. They locked him in to protect him from anticipated pursuers.

He would stay in the basement for hours, and the regular bar activity went on as usual.

The man had major alcohol and other drug addictions. He eventually decided to move to the Southwest to get away from family and friends who were "nagging" him to get help.

Christine tells me the man is now deceased. He "blew his brains out" shortly after the move. The weather gets hot in that part of the country, and it took a while for his body to be found in his trailer. The heat "made his body so bloated that it split open."

He was in his mid-thirties.

Two Men in a Bar

Jeff Burkhart is a bartender at an upscale restaurant where I live in Marin County, California. He wrote a wonderful book a few years ago with the equally wonderful title, *Twenty Years Behind Bars: The Spirited Adventures of a Real Bartender*. He also writes a regular column entitled *Barfly* for our local *Marin Independent Journal* newspaper. I smiled when I read his November 2, 2014 column. I think you will smile, too.

Jeff discusses what happened at his bar one night, the night of a big game watched by patrons on the bar's TV. He overhears a conversation between two men wearing black hats sitting together, men he describes as "Hat Man No. 1" and "Hat Man No. 2." Hat Man No.1 is increasingly agitated about a man he sees sitting at a nearby table, a man looking away from the television screen, which has everyone else transfixed. "That guy over there is staring at me," Hat Man No. 1 says. "He's been staring at me all game. I don't like it." As time passes, Hat Man No. 1 increasingly attributes all sorts of thoughts and feelings to the staring stranger. "I guess he doesn't like sports fans"; "I bet he's mad that sports fans are here at this fancy bar"; "I bet that guy thinks he's better than me"; "I bet I make just as much money as he does"; "I bet I have a nicer car than he does." And so it went, even when his friend, Hat Man No. 2, tells him, "You're imagining things."

Finally, Hat Man No. 1 declares, "Who does he think he is?" He decides to go over to the man to find out "what his problem is." Just then, however, the staring stranger gets up. He reaches under the table for a white cane. Tap-tap-tap, the cane now leads him to the restroom.

Jeff concludes his column by reminding us: **"What we think other people think about us is often more telling than what they actually do."**

*It is not in the stars to hold
our destiny but in ourselves.*

~William Shakespeare

NINA

Nina is a bartender at a popular bar in one of America's most affluent towns. The bar is a near-anomaly in the area. It has operated for decades in the same spot with the same name, and is known as the local dive—nothing fancy about it at all; in fact, happily the opposite. Even though smoking has been banned for years, the smells of ancient cigarettes and alcohol still seep from the flooring and walls. Or maybe it just seems that way.

I like this place and willingly could waste my time in it.

~**William Shakespeare**, *As You Like It*

The Shelter of Bars

The bar is "down-home" in an often not so down-home town, where customers can drink beer (or spirits), shoot pool, listen to the jukebox and watch games on the big screen TVs scattered around the place. Nina has been bartending there for years. "I love my job," she says, especially the "human interaction." During the worst of the recession just a few years ago, "there was a lot of talk [at the bar] about job loss, losing homes, marriage separations and other such maladies.... There was a certain desperateness in people, and one of the few places where they could find solace was the bar. They really longed to forget about their troubles for a while, or at least feel like they weren't alone. So you listen...or simply try to make them laugh. It feels good when you can be there for, sometimes, a perfect stranger."

It is "our job as bartenders to make customers feel comfortable, welcomed and want to come back," Nina continues. Her bar, like so many, often fills up fast, with large disparate groups of people inexplicably forming simultaneously. "I shift into high gear, pick up my pace and focus on the order in which they came and serve them accordingly. I multitask my way up and down the long bar...smiling and greeting each one personally."

Nina adds, "Any seasoned bartender will tell you that they like this. It's a time when we can really put our skills to use and we enjoy getting into the flow of what feels like a well-choreographed dance." Bartending is "not a glamorous job, nor nearly as 'fun' as most people believe it to be." She feels a good bartender makes "it look fun and easy....It definitely takes a certain type of person to be able to do it right and still enjoy it. I happen to be one of those people."

Nina enhances my understanding of how a bar can be a safe haven, a place for people to escape their personal or professional stressors, and simply have fun and relax. The bar can be a great

What Did Uncle Harold Know?

"second home" for them—or even their favorite place to be. The games on TV, the fellowship, the alcohol can at least temporarily lessen worries and re-energize people for the next day. At Nina's type of bar, with its average guy and gal atmosphere, letting down one's guard becomes easier. A bar can serve as a windbreak from the world. If "windbreak" means *shelter from the wind* and *breaking the force of the wind,* it is an apt metaphor for what is best about bars and bartending.

The Vulnerability in Bars

One of Nina's concerns about her job involves the *enabling* of unhealthy behavior. This not only involves the abuse of alcohol, but the manipulations and passive-aggressive actions of both customers and bartenders. Tips provide a powerful carrot and stick.

Nina makes me think of Christine, my first interviewee, who now works one day a week as a bartender, but otherwise has a job helping people with disabilities find employment. Christine describes it this way: "I help the disabled" in one job, then "I help *make* people disabled" at the bar.

Nina targets the flip side of the solace and friendship a bartender provides when she says, "The hard part [is] taking their money....The worst thing is to watch certain people bury themselves even farther by drinking to excess and wasting what little money [some of them have] in booze. In essence, you are contributing to their demise."

She also recognizes that mixed messages can be sent and received between a bartender and customer. "Some of the 'lonelier' people, and often times men, will misinterpret [a female bartender's] kindness as a genuine bond of friendship. That's not to say I don't care or have compassion…but I am not doing it out of friendship….I'm literally getting paid for it….I will most likely have no contact with them outside the bar setting. However, they *will* add me to *their* friends list."

Bartending requires—especially with tips in the balance—constant patience and the willingness to be friendly, polite, and accommodating even when dealing with rude or obnoxious customers. She realizes this is just part of the job, the nature of customer service itself. She and fellow bartenders find relief and joy by sharing customer stories with one another. These "are simply situations that all bartenders go through and gripe about [among themselves] pretty much *every* night. And if they are doing their jobs right, [the bartenders' feelings] will go completely unnoticed *across the wood*."

Nina offers examples of such irritating customer experiences:

- One of her regular customers announced that he only had enough money to cover the cost of his drinks. He would not be tipping her that night.
- Another man asked, "Are your margaritas good here?" She says bartenders often get that question. Such customers may actually mean, "Can you make a margarita the way I want it?" But Nina says bartenders hear their question as, "I see that you are a bartender, which means you know how to make [a variety of] mixed drinks…but I want to know if you actually know what you're doing" before I pay for one I don't like. Nina's story is not the first I've heard of a customer testing a bartender's knowledge and skill in a manner that seems both competitive and condescending.

- One of her regulars interrupted her when she was at her busiest. She says this happens all the time to bartenders, even among (maybe especially among) regulars. They *know* just how busy the bar is, that the bartender needs to concentrate. They say they don't need anything themselves, but still try to engage the busy bartender in conversation: "Are you all alone? Don't you have help?" Nina says, "This may seem…like a concerned customer who is only looking out for you, but to the bartender, they are not only insulting your performance by not seeing the skill and efficiency you are exhibiting, but are…disrupting the very flow of the speed and focus it all requires." They come across like children wanting attention. "In fact, they are not children…[which is] why it's so annoying! Would they think it…helpful if I saw them at their job and stopped them in the middle of what they were doing to tell them it looks like they need help?"

Nina describes our discussion as "what it means to be a bartender." As with any profession, there are positive and negative outcomes, good and bad days. The good clearly outweighs the bad for Nina. She takes pride in her work and the diverse skills it requires. She also feels she is "lucky to have so many cool and friendly customers in a great local bar."

Nina's fantasies also provide laughter and relief on a tough day.

"Are your margaritas good here?"

"No! They're terrible! *Do you still want one?"*

You dreamer, you.

There are two ways of spreading light: To be the candle or the mirror that reflects it.

~Edith Wharton

SPREADING LIGHT

Nina inspires many thoughts about the role of a bartender, about the interactions between bartenders and bar customers. I wonder, once again, what impact Uncle Harold had on the people who frequented his bars and how they influenced him. As we have seen, bars can be places of significant meaning, well beyond what we might first think.

I thought about the influence of people during a family gathering for my nephew, Ryan. He had just graduated from high school. Ryan's 21-year-old brother, Jeremy, who had earned a bachelor's degree in only three years, was in a jubilant mood. So were their friends—friends they had known since infancy. A picture of all five boys was taken, their arms around each other. Eyes in the watching crowd glistened, the babies all grown up. Such good kids, ready for college and careers, ready to take on the world.

I loved learning that Jeremy and Ryan's preschool teacher had recently written them. She said how much it had meant to her to care for them as infants and toddlers. She realized they might not remember her, but she had never forgotten them. She knew she had played an important role in their early development. She was so proud of that, so proud of the boys.

Sometimes we don't realize until years later how someone has shaped and instructed our lives.

I was feeling sentimental as I celebrated with my nephews, their friends, and the rest of my family. Then my friend Bev and the bar she once owned, Aunt Ruby's, popped into my head. I wondered why Bev had chosen that name for her bar. I called her. It just so happens that *all of this* leads to our next bartender tale. It is a wonderful one.

Those who are happiest are those who do the most for others.

~Booker T. Washington

Aunt Ruby's

My friend Bev once owned a bar named *Aunt Ruby's*. I asked her recently if Ruby had been a real person. Ruby had indeed been her aunt, her father's sister, who died a few years ago. Memories of Ruby's unique way of pronouncing words and Southern-type twang clearly delight Bev. Ruby had had a rough life, full of financial hardship and other traumas and tragedies. She was one of those people with limited formal education, but bountiful wisdom. Bev had long been the beneficiary of that wisdom. In Bev's budding adulthood, her Aunt Ruby had unexpectedly reached out to her. She found words that conveyed acute insights into Bev's needs and vulnerabilities, words that offered a foundation of strength and devotion. Bev knew she would one day return such a gift to Aunt Ruby. When she bought the bar, she named it *Aunt Ruby's*. That was the beginning of the gift.

Ruby, by then in her early 70s, had never been on an airplane. She had hardly traveled anywhere. Imagine her feelings when Bev bought her a ticket to fly across the United States to one of the most famous and exciting cities in the world. Imagine a limousine waiting for her, Bev and glasses of champagne inside. Then there was Opening Night at the bar. It was packed. The excited crowd was waiting for the bar's namesake to arrive. Roses and applause greeted Aunt Ruby. And then she jitterbugged the night away, the belle of the ball.

As we appreciate the remaining stories in this book, let us remember all the "Aunt Rubys" in our lives, all the Aunt Rubys all over the world. (I hope you can hear me, Teetie.)

Her finely touched spirit.... Her full nature...spent itself in channels which had no great name on the earth. But the effect of her being on those around her was incalculably diffusive...for the growing good of the world....

~George Eliot, *Middlemarch*

FACES AT THE BAR

Remember Bobbie, the second person I interviewed—the "Fasten your seat belts, here's Bobbie!" bartender? She now returns to us with another shocking story. This story is also deeply moving. I suppose what happened to Bobbie, and the other people you'll soon meet, could have happened in all sorts of settings for all kinds of reasons. As we have seen, however, breathtaking things happen to Bobbie in bars and restaurants.

Bobbie is now in her early sixties. Her first marriage ended in divorce. She and her second husband have been married for seventeen years. Bobbie was unable to get pregnant in either marriage, a great sorrow for both Bobbie and her husbands. People sometimes think of her as a woman without children or grandchildren, as neither a mother nor grandmother.

They are wrong.

Bobbie carries the complicated, emotional history of someone who puts a child up for adoption while an unmarried teenager, and then is never able to conceive children again. How does someone like Bobbie answer people when they ask, "Do you have children, Bobbie?" Depending on the circumstances, her answer might be, "No" (with a silent Yes!) or "Yes" (with a hint of *let's talk about something else.*) Comfort and relief can be felt when transparency—truth-telling—seems appropriate. The full story explains so much.

*Thousands of candles can be
lighted from a single candle,
And the life of the candle will not be
shortened.
Happiness never decreases
by being shared.*

~Buddha

A Mother's Love

Bobbie was a teenager when she got pregnant by her handsome lifeguard boyfriend. He wasn't ready for marriage or fatherhood; she wasn't equipped to handle a child on her own. Bobbie wanted her child to have the best opportunities the circumstances would allow. She ruled out abortion and bravely brought the pregnancy to term, spurred on by her doctor, who said he knew of some fine couples who dreamed of adopting a child.

Bobbie's little girl, ultimately named Emma, was taken by a local adoption agency right after birth. Bobbie gave the agency a letter she hoped would be given to her daughter one day. Bobbie provided loving explanations about the adoption, as well as biographical details, such as her name. She said she hoped they would meet one day.

Have you ever noticed that life is sometimes breathtakingly synchronistic? That the vulnerabilities and strengths and the needs and dreams of people—total strangers even—seem to mesh at just the right time? As if they were meant for each other? So it seemed for Bobbie and a woman named Marie.

Marie and her husband George lived in the same popular beach town where Bobbie grew up. They were anxious to become parents. It seemed inexplicable, so unfair, that Marie just couldn't become pregnant. People sometimes asked if she had kids. The subject was complicated and emotional for Marie. She had gotten pregnant as a teen, an even younger teen than Bobbie. Marie also carried her baby to term and gave birth. In this case, Marie's parents decided they would raise the child. This baby would be the only child Marie ever conceived.

Marie and George were thrilled when a local adoption agency told them they would become the parents of a beautiful newborn girl. They decided to name her Emma. Marie and George and Bobbie were not told they resided in the same town. Thus, the chances over the years of their innocently passing one another on a street, in a store, or at the beach were increasingly likely. Their chances of recognizing a physical connection heightened as Emma grew up. As she developed, Emma's face dramatically resembled Bobbie's. Recognition doubled because Bobbie's twin, Betsy, also lived nearby. Ironically, Bobbie and Betsy are fraternal twins, but no one would guess. Their faces are nearly identical. So, as the years passed, three faces in one town looked increasingly alike. Emma and Bobbie and Betsy: faces of Emma's birth, faces of motherhood.

Synchronistic experiences continued. One of the most popular restaurants and bars in town, and *the very favorite restaurant and bar of Emma and Marie*, just happened to be where Bobbie and Betsy worked, where they bartended and served patrons for years. Think of the likelihood that Bobbie or Betsy, or both, served Emma and Marie, perhaps many times.

Sometimes we don't see what is staring right at us. We are busy, distracted. Recognition is emotional. The mind and heart do pirouettes. Sometimes we move on to other jobs in other locations hundreds of miles away, as Bobbie did. Recognition is then left to those who remain and remember us.

That is how the beautiful baby Emma, all grown up, found Bobbie. That is how Bobbie and Marie, both mothers of Emma, found each other.

Imagine the day when 25-year-old Emma entered her favorite local restaurant once again. This time, a server named Darla stared at her and said, "You look so much like someone I know. She used to work here." Emma smiled, "That happens all the time." She didn't take it seriously; some people just have that kind of face. But Emma added, "I was adopted. What's your friend's name?"

Darla knew Bobbie's newborn daughter had been adopted more than twenty years before.

What a further stroke of luck that the restaurant kept pictures of current and former employees on a wall; that Darla knew Bobbie's maiden name; and that the adoptive parents had indeed given Emma Bobbie's goodbye letter, the letter that contained that name.

Thank you to those who remember us.

Darla told Emma the name of the woman in the picture, the picture Darla now took from the wall. In that instant, Emma knew she was staring at the face of her birth mother.

It didn't take long for Darla to call Bobbie: "I just met your daughter!"

In an instant, lives can change.

Amazement and joy abounded as the news spread. Bobbie and Emma soon met; Bobbie and Marie spoke by telephone. Everyone was respectful of boundaries and potential vulnerabilities, while also celebrating the remarkable reunion.

Emma married a short while later.

Many years have now gone by. Emma and her husband are the proud parents of two teenagers. Over the years, Bobbie has periodically seen Emma and her family, as well as Marie and George. She is grateful. The children know Bobbie as a family friend; Marie is their devoted grandmother.

Emma deeply appreciates both women. She knows what they have meant to her life and what she means to both of them. Her character is a testament to the beautiful life Marie and George gave her. Knowing this warms Bobbie's heart.

Bobbie's story expands our appreciation of what can happen at a bar and restaurant.

I had a mother who gave birth to me and loved me.
I had a mother who adopted me and loved me.

~Unknown Author

The Road Not Taken

Two roads diverged in a yellow wood,
And sorry I could not travel both
And be one traveler, long I stood
And looked down one as far as I could
To where it bent in the undergrowth;

Then took the other, as just as fair,
And having perhaps the better claim,
Because it was grassy and wanted wear;
Though as for that the passing there
Had worn them really about the same,

And both that morning equally lay
In leaves no step had trodden black.
Oh, I kept the first for another day!
Yet knowing how way leads on to way,
I doubted if I should ever come back.

I shall be telling this with a sigh
Somewhere ages and ages hence:
Two roads diverged in a wood, and I—
I took the one less traveled by,
And that has made all the difference.

~Robert Frost

MARK

When I was a kid, I sometimes watched professional wrestling matches on TV. It's been a favorite pastime of many Americans for decades. You can look up "Professional Wrestling" online and read discussions about what parts of the action are staged. Most contend the matches themselves are largely fake, the injuries largely real.

There are multiple books on the subject. One pro, Bret Hart, was born into a family of wrestlers and his book, *Hitman: My Real Life in the Cartoon World of Wrestling,* highlights the staged, entertaining aspects of the sport, but also the very real dangers of concussions and other serious injuries inherent in performing stunts that are "credible and exciting."

Some wrestlers make names for themselves; others become superstars such as Hulk Hogan.

Referees also have a following. The best are great entertainers themselves. They whip around the ring, creating drama and excitement while making their calls.

I meet a man named Mark. He worked for one of the most famous referees decades ago. Mark was a college student back then and bartended at the referee's popular restaurant in the Midwest. It was Mark's first job. He knew the referee and restaurant owner was considered by many the best of all the wrestling referees. Online posts from fans to this day refer to him as "respected," "loved" and "one of the good guys." "Grandfatherly" is a term used by a man recalling his family's happy weekly meals at the restaurant, where the owner made them feel so welcome.

Many wrestling aficionados might relish such close proximity to such a fine, nationally recognized person. Mark is deeply troubled by the memory. He chooses to tell me what happened for this book.

HATRED:
*The coward's revenge
for being intimidated.*

~Hosea Ballou

Cowardice and Courage

Mark tells me that this popular man, this nationally known referee, who so welcomed some people, "wouldn't serve black people in his restaurant." He told Mark, "I got nothing against blacks. It's just the niggers I can't stand!"

Mark continues, "There was a package liquor store at the entrance to the restaurant that served the mostly black community. It was my job to work it if no one else was available. In the three years I worked at [the restaurant bar], I saw two black people served...both were on the City Council. One day a young black man walked past me through the package store into the restaurant. [The referee] grabbed the young man and hustled him back into the package store, telling him that he needed a proper suit jacket to dine at our establishment. Suitably ticked off, the young man stormed out, loudly proclaiming he'd come back—which he did. At which point, [the referee] kicked him out again because he wasn't wearing a tie." When the referee asked Mark why he'd allowed the man to enter the restaurant, Mark said he "couldn't see anything wrong with him, so I let him pass."

Now middle-aged, Mark says, "In retrospect, I wish I'd had the courage to tell him that I thought his actions were not only morally reprehensible, but legally suspect as well. But I needed the job, so I bit my tongue and merely tried to undermine what I saw as a racist policy. From that night on, I avoided working in the package store, fearing retribution from any local man who had wrongfully been refused service in our restaurant."

I am moved by the bravery Mark displayed as a college student, and also by his concern decades later that his actions weren't brave enough. Mark taught me another way a bartender can reach out to customers.

His conscience and actions make me think of the following:

The Man in the Arena

It is not the critic who counts; not the man who points out how the strong man stumbles, or where the doer of deeds could have done better. The credit belongs to the man who is actually in the arena, whose face is marred by dust and sweat and blood; who strives valiantly; who errs, who comes up short again and again, because there is no effort without error and shortcoming; but who does actually strive to do the deeds; who knows great enthusiasms, the great devotions; who spends himself in a worthy cause, who at the best knows in the end the triumph of high achievement, and who at the worst, if he fails, at least fails while daring greatly, so that his place shall never be with those cold and timid souls who neither know victory nor defeat.

~Theodore Roosevelt

It is from numberless diverse acts of courage and belief that human history is shaped. Each time a man stands up for an ideal, or acts to improve the lot of others, or strikes out against injustice, he sends forth a tiny ripple of hope....

~Robert F. Kennedy
**Day of Affirmation Address
Cape Town University
South Africa
June 6, 1966**

ANN & XENA

Just when I thought my book covered the gist of what goes on in a bar, I met two sisters from the Midwest, Ann and Xena. Ann bought a bar in the mid-1970s when she was a rookie at almost everything a bar owner needs to know. Several years later, Xena asked if she could bartend for her sister, a new endeavor for her, as well. Running a successful business is tough; their task was tougher. This was a gay bar in the 1970s and '80s, a time when homophobic feelings were rampant. It didn't take long for the two sisters to demonstrate their skills and take on the town.

They became stars in their own show.

Ann is retired now; Xena is a nurse. Both bars Ann ultimately owned are closed. People all over town feel the loss—men and women; gay and straight; top-notch professionals; blue collar workers; and street toughs—wistfully remember the good old days of Ann and Xena.

It's time for you to meet these sisters.

A teacher affects eternity; he can never tell where his influence stops.

~Henry Adams

Two Sisters Teach Each Other and a Town

I am intrigued to meet two bartender sisters from the Midwest, one lesbian, the other straight. The straight one, who wants to be known as "Xena" (the fearless warrior) for this book, has two grown children and has just become a grandmother. She left her bartending career many years ago and is now a nurse.

Xena started her bartending career in the early 1980s at her sister Ann's gay bar, a bar Ann bought in 1976. Owning a bar of any sort was a new experience for Ann. However, her natural business smarts and welcoming, entertaining personality compensated from the get-go for any rookie challenges. Her sister had the same winning traits. Xena, who had never bartended, asked Ann if she'd hire her. Ann responded, "Make me a scotch with a splash." Xena grabbed a glass, poured some scotch, turned on the faucet, slapped the water. It made a perfect dive. A drink was made, a career born.

Business had boomed from the start, and now Xena was attracting a lively crowd. Some bartenders just have the touch. Gay and straight people became regulars. The scene was often uproariously fun and happy. Fear, anger, and jealousy also came calling. When that happened, other patrons responded with tribal loyalty and protectiveness. The underbelly of any drinking establishment can be raw, with alcohol the primary culprit. Horrified patrons galvanized when a woman without an ID lunged at Xena with a sharp instrument. Xena had refused to serve her. Without word or hesitation, they pounced on the woman and got the knife. "I've got your back" was the unspoken motto of this and many other bars.

Ann had encountered business start-up problems from the beginning, and not just the usual ones. The town erupted at the idea of having a gay establishment in its midst. This was 1976, when anti-gay feelings were widespread and openly gay bars few. Some lesbians even objected to the presence of straight women at their new bar. Ann recalls local toughs—straight, macho men—who figured they could scare the dykes and effeminate gay male bartenders out of town. Fights ensued. Ann chuckles recalling the fight that knocked out bartender Doug's front tooth. Doug would be the first to call himself "a queen." He certainly earned a crown as he bloodied and trounced the detractors.

Virulent anti-gay sentiments finally settled down. Patrons—men and women, gay and straight—drank, ate, and danced until the wee hours of the morning. Locals still wistfully speak about the bar, which has been closed for years now. They remember other people and other dramas that once filled Ann's first and then second gay bar in the same town.

Ann tells me about a regular, a forensic chemist, who was all over the news and then sent to prison for drug tampering. The chemist also pulled a fast one or two on Ann. She wore very short hair, men's suits, and flashed money in her male wallet. She was tough and aggressive. When Ann raised the price of drinks by a nickel, the woman started a boycott by holding Happy

Hour at her nearby house. Ann's voice of reason ultimately prevailed. The chemist eventually went on trial for diluting and siphoning off cocaine. She claimed the charges were a set up, an effort to "out" her as gay to her employer. Her defense failed.

Ann dealt with other illegal schemes. She noticed on certain days at certain times certain customers would wear white hats or feathers. This meant drug action in the restroom. Time to call the cops.

Then she shut down the "straws in a glass" thefts of one of her own bartenders. A good bartender gets a feel for when it's smart to "buy" a drink for a customer—a thank you for the patronage of a regular or as a friendly gesture for someone else. They ring up the transaction as a No Sale to account for the inventory reduction that does not have an accompanying payment. Bar owners expect and encourage such behavior up to a point, knowing such gestures can ultimately grow business.

Some employees decide to help themselves instead. Ann noticed one of her bartenders periodically added a straw to a nearby glass. She wondered why and secretly watched. The bartender added a straw to the glass when she rang up some of her No Sales. The straws represented the drinks that were actually *not* No Sales because she charged these customers. The straws helped her keep track of the money she would pay herself from the cash register at the end of the evening when all the bartenders had to settle their day's transactions.

Ann figured out the scheme and handled it with her usual aplomb. Imagine the bartender's thoughts when she saw Ann walk over to the glass and stuff it with straws. "Do we have any questions?" A warning issued, a lesson learned, a job saved.

No wonder Ann ultimately became an employment professional.

Now it's time to introduce you to Miss Xena's Romper Room. Ann marveled at the uptick in customers and sales on Saturday afternoons, already a popular time. What in the world was her sister doing? Even Xena was amazed. Xena was shopping for her young children one day—coloring books and crayons, jacks, Play-Doh. It struck her to take these items to the bar. Would customers love it or think it ridiculous to institute "Miss Xena's Romper Room," complete with "Miss Xena, may I please have a drink?" and not be served until a picture was colored, popcorn was strung, or a similar task completed? The idea took off big-time. Sophisticated businessmen, doctors, lawyers, blue-collar workers, and street toughs seemed to get a charge out of it. Even some of the initially reluctant became converts. "Okay, give me some that Play-Doh."

Are grown-ups still children at heart? Did Xena's game bring back memories of carefree, silly, and fun times? It seemed a vehicle for producing those results, for providing relief from facades and inhibitions, for delivering people from their problems and worries.

Both Ann and Xena remark about the emotional comfort of bars, about how personalities can even transform—and not just because of alcohol or the feeling of anonymity. Otherwise quiet and serious customers seem to want and need to let go. They will sing and dance up a storm, gleefully play Miss Xena's Romper Room. A bar can seem a private, freeing oasis. No one expects to be judged. People just assume the bartender, like one's attorney or priest, can be trusted with secrets. Ann says customers often spoke to her about their troubles, about affairs or other hardships. They needed someone to listen to them. She hopes she was helpful. Xena had the same experience. She sometimes discussed her own problems with customers. She feels the trust and vulnerability she exhibited led to mutually meaningful exchanges.

Singing and comedic skits became part of life at both of Ann's bars. Ann and Xena often starred in them. The crowd loved it and many participated. Ann also hired people to perform. She and her business partner, Beth, once hired an opera singer. Everyone was entranced by her voice when a fight broke out between two men. A furious Beth bellowed, "We try to have some class in here and all you do is fuck it up."

Ann and Xena show us, once again, the vibrant, often moving, and also disturbing world inside bars. We see the ecstasy and agony of the human spirit, the mysteries and complexities and vulnerabilities. I am reminded of these quotations:

We are all alike, on the inside.

~Mark Twain

*People are like stained glass windows.
They sparkle and shine when the sun is out,
but when the darkness sets in,
their true beauty is revealed only if there is light from within.*

~Elisabeth Kubler-Ross

ONE SUMMER
IN MAINE

Just when I thought I had finished writing my book, memories of my summer in Maine in 1971 suddenly took hold. I knew there were interesting bartender stories from that period, but the rest of what I wanted to say seemed out-of-kilter with the book's theme. Then I flashed to the similarities between Leroy, from bartender Christine's recollections, and Charlie Walls, from mine. They were different men in different circumstances. But each wrought tenderness from twenty-something Christine and me, a tenderness that might escape or mystify others. Then additional experiences from that summer unfolded from there.

I finally realized these memories beautifully capture what this book is about: human nature, the human condition, the stuff of life. Sometimes we see those elements most acutely displayed in a bar, but they are the wonders and sorrows and passions and lessons that are always part of our lives.

Please come along with me to Maine.

*The greatest glory in living lies
not in never falling,
but in rising every time we fall.*

~Confucius

Mount Desert Island, Maine

The state of Maine has always held a romantic quality for me. Deep family roots from both my parents are there, and memories of countless happy times. My father received a Ph.D. in French from the University of Iowa in 1953 and anticipated a career as a college professor in Maine or some other East Coast state. That trajectory changed when scouts from what would ultimately be known as Humboldt State University in Arcata, California, enticed my parents westward.

The move brought the glamour—and the distance—of the big state of California to our Maine relatives. The cost of flying and the driving distance with five children meant several years between our visits to Maine. When we did get together, everything sparkled for me. I thought my relatives were just the best, that everything in Maine was laughter and lobsters, boating and swimming, and visiting beautiful resort towns such as Bar Harbor on Mount Desert Island. Bar Harbor was located about an hour from Bangor, where most of my relatives lived.

Have you ever been to Mount Desert Island? It is the largest island on the coast of Maine, 108 square miles, and is a place of exquisite beauty. Acadia National Park and Cadillac Mountain, with its spectacular view of the sunrise, draw millions of tourists. My fondest memories are of sitting on the craggy reddish rocks that border the shimmering and sometimes rollicking sea. I can't tell you the number of times my relatives and I found our favorite spot and sat on those rocks, eating crackers and cheese, feeding seagulls, taking in the air.

Mount Desert Island consists of four towns, one of which is Bar Harbor. A second town, Mount Desert, is comprised of six villages. Northeast Harbor and Seal Harbor are probably the best known of the six. But it is the village of Otter Creek that I will be telling you about. Both famous Bar Harbor and little Otter Creek significantly marked my life, especially during the summer of 1971. I will be telling you all sorts of tales, including of course bartender tales, from those two places. You might call them my very own "coming of age" stories.

I spent "my junior year abroad" at my parents' alma mater, the University of Maine in Orono, just outside Bangor. I roomed with my cousin Debbie, who grew up nearby. Debbie and I decided to try out waitressing during the accompanying summer of 1971. Bar Harbor was our dream destination. We nailed it! Both of us got waitress jobs at a new restaurant opening smack dab in the center of that town. We rented a room for the summer at the YWCA. That began our adventure as *inhabitants* of Bar Harbor, Maine.

Bar Harbor

To rekindle Bar Harbor memories, I Google "Geddy's Bar, Bar Harbor, Maine" and am flabbergasted by what pops up. Ha! "The Legend of Geddy's." The story is indeed about the man who romanced me for a few weeks during the summer of 1971, Gerry ("Geddy") Mitchell. Gerry was a life-long Bar Harbor resident, age 25. Charismatic and a whirling dervish, he acted as though he owned the town. He treated Debbie and me to drinks and fun at various Bar Harbor places (sometimes popping behind the bar and making us drinks at establishments that weren't even his). I'd heard that in 1974, Gerry bought the "surfside saloon" on Main Street that housed one of those bars and named it, predictably, Geddy's. I shake my head over this "Legend" story, in which I recognize talents I figured Gerry would display one day, and also behaviors I never witnessed but do not doubt. Here's the story:

"Long before Geddy's became a world-famous watering hole, this historic building was home to a dingy waterfront dive avoided by locals, abhorred by the tourist bureau, and frequented by all the shady characters that drifted by. Locals referred to it as the 'hellhole of Hancock County.' Gerry 'Geddy' Mitchell bought this surfside saloon in 1974 and decided to change the clientele completely. He was a bouncer, merchant marine and a sailor, and he was as tough as the crowd in the bar. The transformation began.

"In ten days, he threw out 56 people, knocking out 27 of them, and putting seven others into the hospital. When he went to toss out the 57th, an unhappy ejectee shot him in the back with a 12-gauge shotgun. Geddy survived and prospered, and turned the bar into a Mecca for tourists and a venue for some great music. Entertainers such as Bonnie Raitt, Wynton Marsalis, Taj Mahal, Pure Prairie League, Livingston Taylor, Arlo Guthrie, and Los Lobos performed to packed crowds, and the legend of Geddy's grew. But in 1987, Geddy's sailor's blood stirred again. He sold the bar and sought out adventure elsewhere."

The new owners transformed Geddy's into a family-friendly restaurant and bar, which is advertised to this day as "World-famous....If you haven't been to Geddy's, then you haven't been to Bar Harbor."

I ask my cousin if she remembers that little downstairs saloon on Main Street as the hellhole just described. We both remember it as having way too much cigarette smoke, but otherwise filled with fun regulars. We even took Aunt Minnie, Debbie's mother, there! Maybe it changed after 1971, or perhaps we were naïve 20 year olds (the legal drinking age in Maine) who only saw, or dealt with, what was on the surface of the place. (This makes me wonder what Uncle

Harold might have known about Mob connections in Vegas and elsewhere.)

Debbie and I have nothing but happy memories of Bar Harbor. The famous Mary Jane Restaurant was near the Y and we often dropped by in the evenings. In the past, it was a favorite for dinner when our family visited Bar Harbor for the day. Now, this was Debbie's and my local place, almost as if we were townies. The bartender—Mike?—seemed to enjoy us. He overheard Debbie wondering about a new popular drink, The Harvey Wallbanger, and surprised her with one on the house. She nearly gagged after her first sip, but faked it for a while out of sensitivity to his feelings. (The drink went in the toilet the minute he turned his attentions elsewhere.) Mike was a fun bartender. He made us feel special.

The Gilded Age

To really understand Bar Harbor—in fact, all of Mount Desert Island—you need to understand what Mark Twain called "The Gilded Age," where fabulous wealth was accumulated by a handful of pioneering men. Think Rockefeller, Vanderbilt, Astor, J.P. Morgan, Henry Ford, men whose fortunes were built in the late 19th and early 20th centuries from oil, railroads, the fur trade, shipping, banking and automobiles. Mount Desert Island, with its serenity and beauty and distance from the hustle and hassle of big cities—and its appealing climate—created a summer escape from New York, Philadelphia, Boston and other sweltering cities. These men and their families built luxurious estates overlooking the ocean in various parts of the Island.

The Island offered hotels and inns for those of prominence or means who did not own a house there, but sought a luxurious summertime getaway. The still-fabulous Asticou Inn in Northeast Harbor often served that purpose. My mother remembers her grandmother, Elizabeth Boutelle Palmer, the daughter of Congressman Boutelle, enjoying many summers at the Asticou (or a similar) Inn.

The life of the "gilded" people of Mount Desert Island filled East Coast newspapers of the day. Their receptions, house parties, dances, and movements through town in chauffeured cars were legendary. They lent a sparkling aura to Bar Harbor, and to the entire Island. My older Maine relatives tell me the spirit of these people suggested "old money." The people were, or seemed, educated, cultured, philanthropic, comfortable and confident in their own skins. The public response to them was one of vicarious delight and admiration.

The Bar Harbor Fire of 1947

That glorious golden life received a horrifying blow in mid-October 1947. Somehow—maybe the drought combined with human folly—a fire was ignited in Bar Harbor. It raged and raced for two weeks, until 17,000 acres all over the Island were destroyed. Homes and businesses were ravaged. Most of the grand estates were in ruins; many were never rebuilt. The charred remains of stone foundations and other artifacts now serve as reminders of the Island's golden age. It was an age that passed nearly seventy years ago due to economic losses and changing priorities caused by the Great Depression, World War II, and of course that dreadful fire.

Hamilton Hill

My cousin and I can attest to the drama of seeing these ruins. Locals told us if we hiked up nearby Hamilton Hill, we could see what was left of the once magnificent estate of J.P. Morgan's daughter, Juliet Pierpont Morgan, and her husband, William Pierson Hamilton (the great-grandson of

Alexander Hamilton). We set forth one evening, a fresh loaf of bread and a hunk of cheese in hand, plus a bottle of white wine. It took our breath away when we saw what was left and to imagine what must have been. We could discern remnants of the foundation of a huge house and see gorgeous tile work surrounding what must have been a large swimming pool. The property afforded a spectacular water view, made all the more impressive when the Bluenose Ferry from Nova Scotia appeared. It was lit up like a jewel.

Debbie and I could easily imagine violins playing as elegantly dressed men and women danced the night away at this glorious house on a hill.

Goodbye to Our First Bar Harbor Job

Debbie and I loved Bar Harbor, but business at the new restaurant wasn't as anticipated. The owners over-hired and had to let us go. We didn't worry. Debbie landed another waitress job at a nearby popular bar and restaurant. She started raking in the tips. Someone (probably Gerry Mitchell) told me a man named Charlie Walls was about to open his dream café in nearby Otter Creek and needed a waitress. I'd never heard of Otter Creek, but decided to give it a try.

Charlie only served lunch (and beer) at his new place, a place he appropriately named, Charlie's Lunch.

Charlie's Lunch: Otter Creek, Maine

If Bar Harbor was familiar— exciting and bustling with tourists—Otter Creek was its opposite. To be honest, all I saw of this small village with its few hundred residents was while I was going back and forth to work. From what I read online now, Otter Creek is still quiet, but campers and others enjoy it. I smile when I read there is a Walls Street in the village. It apparently honors the Walls family, whose members have lived in Otter Creek for generations. Charlie must have been part of that clan. Then I find an obituary for a Charles N. Walls of Otter Creek, Maine, who died at age 84 in 2004. I know this is my Charlie when the short summation of the man's life mentions his enjoyment of yard sales. My Charlie Walls was proud of what he got at yard sales. He told me opening a place that served lunch in Otter Creek was a long-standing goal. Bit by bit, he built up a stash of goods for his future café. He got dishes and plates, as well as cups and saucers, at yard sales, items he made sure had no chips or cracks. He found silverware, too. In early summer 1971, Charlie's Lunch was finally ready for business. Charlie Walls was the owner, chef, and beer bartender. I was the sole waitress.

Business was bad, and never got better, during my month-long tenure. I might have gone out of my mind with boredom (and virtually no tips on top of minimal hourly pay) if I hadn't had such tender feelings toward Charlie and his dream.

I also occupied myself by observing him, as if I knew I would one day write about him. He was straight out of Central Casting. In his 50s, with short white hair, Charlie always needed a shave. He was a bit stooped, but lanky and muscular. I think he was a carpenter, but seemed more a man of the sea—a lobsterman, maybe. He'd seen his share of the outdoors. A lit cigarette dangled from his lips most of the day. It stayed there when he talked. In fact, Charlie was one of those guys who seldom use their fingers to flick cigarette ashes; gravity or the wind can handle that task.

Although bartending was his job, Charlie showed me how to pull the tap handle and hold a glass for an appropriate pour of beer. Not a beer drinker myself, I thought the foam on top looked like the best part. He gave me lessons on how much of a "head" to allow. To this day, I can say this: whether the beer head is big or small, the beer is in a can, on tap, light or dark—there is one thing that is always wrong with beer as far as I'm concerned: you just can't get the beer out of beer.

Beer lovers of course disagree, especially on a hot day. I remember a particularly warm afternoon when a middle-aged man entered Charlie's Lunch looking for a cool one. He was our only customer. I knew he was a prominent Bangor businessman. He and Charlie got to talking. Charlie's muscular arm pulled the tap handle and the man took a happy gulp. As Charlie's smoke billowed over the bar, the man explained how his doctor and his wife had been nagging him to get some sort of operation. He told Charlie with a proud guffaw he'd struck a deal with them: he would have the operation if they'd promise a cold six-pack the minute he came to. They promised. Charlie smiled and nodded. Then he chuckled and took another puff.

Goodbye to My Second Job

As you might expect, Charlie had to let me go. It had been about a month and things just weren't happening at Charlie's Lunch. He took me aside one day and told me, as he looked away—eye contact was never his strong suit anyway—he couldn't afford me and felt his business might not make it to the end of the season. He thanked me and said he was sorry. I thanked him, personally relieved, but sad for him.

Charlie could never get my name right. I'd say, "It's Jenny" and he'd say, "Okay, Jeanie." I'd say, "There's no 's' in my last name, it's Wood," and his handwritten paycheck would almost always include an "s." The bank didn't care. I decided I didn't either. So when Charlie handed me my final paycheck, I knew it would make me smile. The check was folded in half. I didn't open it until I got back to Bar Harbor. It read: "Jeanie Woods. $15.00. Fiveteen."

The sweetest fiveteen dollars I've ever made.

Life Lessons and a Fond Farewell

It's a good thing I loved my life on Mount Desert Island and believed a good job awaited me. Wow! Here I go again. I knew I needed to make up for lost time money-wise. Hourly pay for waitresses was nominal, so receiving tips became critical.

My quest for a waitress job at any popular Bar Harbor restaurant (with an active bar) began.

Excellent tips were almost guaranteed, plus I loved the atmosphere of such places. Everybody seemed so relaxed and happy. This was summertime in Bar Harbor, Maine: cocktails and lobsters, after-dinner drinks and laughter. My kind of place—especially as a diner!

Late summer searches failed to yield that job. Instead, I became a waitress at a very, very busy breakfast-lunch-dinner restaurant on nearby Cottage Street, with an ice cream and milkshake take-out service. (No cocktails.) That job taught me anyone who handles all those different tasks, at an endless frantic pace, and keeps even difficult customers happy, is one sharp cookie. I worked at this job until the end of August, when it was time to return to college in California.

What I remember most about that final job occurred the morning of my first breakfast shift. I had to be at the restaurant by 5AM, which meant walking the streets of Bar Harbor at 4:45AM. There was not a single sound, not a single person or car moving on the streets that morning. It was as if everyone and everything on the Island was sound asleep, except for me and two seagulls I spotted on a rooftop above. We eyed each other. I smiled but then looked away and decided to walk extra quietly. It seemed I might be encroaching on their world. What must birds perceive? They look down on all the activity in the world all day, all the sights and sounds. Maybe they know—but we don't realize—there is a brief period of time in a small island town when all the action and noise dissipates and then disappears. Just for a while. But the birds remain; they are still there. Maybe this is their moment. Maybe this is the time when the world is theirs.

*Be happy for this moment.
This moment is your life.*

~Omar Khayyam

LAST CALL

How did we do, Uncle Harold? Do you have any inkling that you and I just wrote a book? We never even met while you were alive, but you were at my side the whole time I wrote. I hope we recreated your world. All the bartenders and bar patrons I interviewed taught me so much. I thank them for both of us. Did we miss anything, Uncle Harold? I hope we captured the essence of a bartender's career: the gaiety and camaraderie and stress relief; the dangers and mind-games and insecurities; the deceit and desperation; the loyalty and kindness and protectiveness; the happiest of people in the happiest of times. A bartender's world is a microcosm of life, juiced to its heights and depths.

I asked my mother the other day what she thought your reaction would be to this book. "Oh, he was such a humble man. He would have been overwhelmed." She guessed your Irish eyes would be filled with sentimental tears.

You knew Frank Sinatra and Nat King Cole and presided among other luminaries as well. Every family member says the same thing about you, "Oh, I just loved Uncle Harold." I'm sorry we never met. We lived and worked in different regions of the country, and you left this world just as I realized how much I wanted to meet you, to talk to you.

So I talked to you through this book. Do you know I went to the current Copacabana in Times Square several months ago? A Saturday night, 10PM. They were closed! "We're open on Tuesday," someone yelled. Imagine! Not like your days, Uncle Harold.

You are a star now. I have loved writing our book. Our work is done and I miss you already. Will you send me a sign, Uncle Harold? I'll watch for twinkling Irish eyes from where you now reside, forever in the sky.

Acknowledgments

How can I express my gratitude to those who encouraged me to write this book and who shared their bartending experiences and observations with me?

Profound thanks to: Lee, Christine, Bobbie, Mrs. Vance, Monica, Jeff, Nina, Bev, Mark, Ann, and Xena. Thank you for the trust you placed in me. Your contributions were magnificent.

I deeply appreciate the support, contributions, and suggestions of my cousin and cousin-in-law, Debbie and Jim Mallar (thanks for all the great times, Debbie!); my fabulous aunts, Mary ("Minnie") Mitchell Graffam and Betsy Mitchell Savage; Cindy Moran; Carolyn La Fontaine; Kevin and Fran Atkins; Micheline Rourke; Jeff Traynor; Gerri Alaniz; Pat Hayman; Dennis Madsen; Nora and Bill Conway; Richard Spitzer; and Jeff Burkhart. You spurred me on just when I needed it.

Cynthia Stanley, I can't find the words.

Jennifer Wood

In addition to my profound thanks to Vice President Joe Biden, Senator Edmund Muskie, and Vice President Walter Mondale, my heartfelt thanks to the people in Washington whose impact on my life has been so meaningful: Madeleine Albright, Bernard Asbell, Wes Barthelmes, Kevin Cash, Leslie Finn, Barbara Gamarekian, Susan Holloway, David Kennedy, Chris Matthews, Frances Miller, Suzanne Salinger, Dolores Stover, Joe Velletri and Arnot Walker. The inspiration I received from each of you made this book possible. Many of you left this world way too soon. You meant the world to me.

Sometimes unexpected people and unexpected situations played important roles in the development of the book. Last year, I decided to Google the name of a long-lost friend. Her joyous response inspired a "go for it, take a chance" spirit. Thank you, Patty Webster. This led to striking genealogical gold. From my perch in California, I found the name of a woman in Maine who seemed to be a distant relative. I knew if my hunches were correct, pieces of a family mystery could be solved. I phoned the woman. She answered. Hello, Angeline Ferris! What fun we've had putting our family puzzle from the early 1800s together. Angie had no idea she was related to the Boutelles of Maine (my family). But as the keeper of *her* family's historical papers, she discovered a picture of my great-great-great grandmother, Lucy Ann Curtis Boutelle. Lucy was the mother of Civil War hero and U.S. Congressman Charles Addison Boutelle, my great-great grandfather. We learned Lucy was the sister of *Angie's* great-great grandfather, renowned shipmaster Captain John Curtis, for whom the Curtis Public Library in Brunswick, Maine is named. No one in my family, at least in recent history, had ever seen a picture of Lucy. Angie then sent a picture of her own mother sitting on a boat decades ago. Her resemblance to *my* mother is stunning. The DNA of third cousins, once removed, shines through.

What does all this have to do with writing the book? Well, nothing and everything. I learned to: follow hunches, assert yourself, make the call, be persistent. Be curious and ask questions. Fight against fear and embarrassment. Dare to make mistakes. Sometimes the payoff is so beautiful. Thank you, Angeline Ferris. My father, the late and beloved Frank Wood, would relish our efforts and discoveries. He was our family genealogist. I've now caught the genealogy bug, Dad. Your torch is ablaze!

The enthusiasm of my sisters and brothers and their partners gave me the confidence and courage to proceed. Thank you so much, Cathy and Don Andrews; Mitch and Deborah Wood; Kent Wood; and Liz and Darryl Lawrence. Special thanks to my niece, Elianna Spitzer, for her flash drive wizardry and to my nephew, Jeremy Lawrence, for the beautiful words at the end of the book.

My mother, Ann Boutelle Mitchell Wood, was immeasurably helpful to me. Your belief in the project, Mom, and gentle and jovial nudging along the way—"I won't be alive forever!"—kept me going when energy and confidence waned. You added in such a special way to my understanding of Uncle Harold and what this book might mean to him. You gave context and meaning to the childhood world that was once his and his brother James's. I feel an even greater appreciation of the marriage and accomplishments of your treasured parents, my treasured grandparents, James Edward Mitchell and Elizabeth Boutelle Palmer Mitchell.

What Did Uncle Harold Know?

The support, advice, and enthusiasm of my life partner, Betty Hirschfeld, were pivotal from beginning to end. Your enjoyment of the book as I wrote it meant more than I can convey. You burnished My Moxie and made all the difference. I couldn't have done it without you, my Betty.

Finally, a seeming miracle arrived shortly after I finished writing the book. I felt at a total loss as to how to proceed to the publishing part. Then a friend named Lynne Arkin, who wrote and published a book last year, guided me toward several sources of publishing assistance. One of them just happened to be the self-publishing expert known as *The Wonderlady*, Ruth Schwartz. Editor, proofreader, guide, mentor, she is a "Book Midwife." How lucky to have found you, Ruth. Many thanks, Lynne.

Special thanks as well to Sam Barry, Author Services Liaison for Book Passage, a wonderful bookstore next to my office, for his expertise and guidance.

Here's to you, Harold Joseph Mitchell.

Notes

To verify and supplement information provided by the contributors to this book, the author conducted Google and Yahoo searches as follows:

HAROLD MITCHELL
"Original Copacabana, New York City"
"Original Sands Hotel, Las Vegas"

CHRISTINE
"A heart that can recognize without aid of the eyes..." is a verse from a poem the Irish Ambassador to the United States, Thomas P. Kiernan, recited to President Kennedy in 1961, to honor the birth of John F. Kennedy, Jr. According to the book, *Johnny, We Hardly Knew Ye*, Ambassador Kiernan asked the President "for permission to recite, from memory, some verses written by an Irish poet friend thirty years earlier to celebrate the birth of his own son, Colm Patrick." The verses were published in newspapers and magazines of the day and then, in 1970, were included in that book (written by Kenneth P. O'Donnell

and David F. Powers, with Joe McCarthy; Little, Brown and Company).

BOBBIE
"David Allen Rundle"
"Quotations about birth and adoptive mothers"—see quote by Unknown Author in FACES IN THE BAR section.

MONICA
"Auburn, California"
"Little Girl Lost by Joan Merriam"
"Murder of Anna Brackett, Auburn, CA"
"Douglas Scott Mickey Case"

MARK
"Professional Wrestling"

ONE SUMMER IN MAINE
"Charles Walls Otter Creek, Maine"
"Otter Creek, Maine"
"Bar Harbor, Maine 1947 Fire"
"Geddy's Bar Harbor, Maine"/"The Legend of Geddy's"
"Acadia National Park"
"Mount Desert Island, Maine Rockefeller"

Telephone consultation with the Bar Harbor Historical Society (to confirm the Hamilton Hill/Alexander Hamilton & J.P. Morgan family connection). July 2015.

About the Author

Jennifer Wood served as Joe Biden's first intern at the U.S. Senate, and later became a Legislative Correspondent and research assistant for Senator Edmund S. Muskie. She then served on the White House Staff of Vice President Walter F. Mondale, where she coordinated logistics for his domestic and foreign travels. Her career has focused on behavioral health in recent years. This is her first book.

She and her partner enjoy their homes in Mill Valley, California and New York City.

www.ingramcontent.com/pod-product-compliance
Lightning Source LLC
Chambersburg PA
CBHW022227010526
44113CB00033B/639